Original title:
Velveted Strings Amid the Faerie Span

Author: Lan Donne
ISBN HARDBACK: 978-1-80559-434-5
ISBN PAPERBACK: 978-1-80559-933-3

The Song of Dreaming Dusk

The sun dips low, a golden sigh,
Whispers hush as the shadows lie.
Stars awaken in the twilight's gleam,
Night's woven fabric begins to dream.

A gentle breeze in the fading light,
Carries tales of day to the night.
Crickets chirp their soft refrain,
Nature hums in a sweet domain.

Clouds drift slowly, painted in hues,
Pink and purple, with evening's muse.
The world exhales, it starts to rest,
In the arms of dusk, it feels blessed.

Reflections dance on the still pond's face,
Mirroring stars in their silver lace.
Moonbeams cast a tender glow,
Guiding dreams where the heart can go.

As shadows lengthen, and silence grows,
The song of dusk in the twilight flows.
In every heart, a secret sigh,
Beneath the vast and starlit sky.

Cadence of Whimsical Whispers

In the garden where dreams play,
Soft echoes dance in the breeze.
Colors twirl in light's soft sway,
Whispers float like honeyed tease.

Petals flutter, secrets shared,
Joyful laughter fills the air.
Nature's heartbeat, unpaired,
Each moment, a gentle prayer.

Moonbeams weave a silver thread,
Stars wink in a playful glow.
Where the heart and spirit tread,
Magic blossoms, free to flow.

Time stands still in twilight's embrace,
Every shadow softly sings.
In this enchanted, sacred space,
Life unfolds on silver wings.

So let the whispers lead you near,
To the paths of wonder's song.
In the cadence, feel no fear,
For in dreams, we all belong.

Twilight Rhapsody in the Green Haven

As twilight cloaks the sky in hue,
The world holds its breath for a while.
In the green haven, magic's brew,
Sunset paints each moment with style.

Gentle breezes stir the leaves,
With secrets carried from afar.
Nature weaves the tales she cleaves,
Beneath the watchful evening star.

Crickets serenade the night,
Their melodies, a soothing balm.
In the dim, they find the light,
A harmony, peaceful and calm.

Violet shadows kiss the ground,
While fireflies spark to greet the dark.
In this haven, dreams are found,
Igniting each heart with a spark.

So linger here in twilight's glow,
Let the rhapsody softly take flight.
In this embrace, all will know,
Magic lives in each gentle night.

Secrets Woven in Celestial Melodies

Whispers rise on gossamer threads,
Carried high to the starry dome.
Each note, a wish that gently bled,
In the quiet of night's sweet home.

Harmonies wrapped in silken light,
Echo softly through cosmic seas.
Where shadows dance with pure delight,
And time drifts with the cosmic breeze.

Galaxies twirl in sync and grace,
Each twinkle a tale yet to tell.
In this vast and endless space,
Music weaves its enchanting spell.

Melodies brush the moon's soft face,
While dreams are strung like pearls on strings.
In this universe, hold your place,
Become the song that softly sings.

So close your eyes, let the stars guide,
In celestial rhythms, find your peace.
In the cosmos, where wonder will bide,
Feel the secrets never cease.

Flourish of the Faerie Orchestra

In hidden glades where magic thrives,
The faerie orchestra takes flight.
With instruments made from nature's lives,
They play beneath the silver light.

Trumpets blow with whispers sweet,
Flutes trill like the morning dew.
In the daisy's dance, the rhythms beat,
The melodies are fresh and new.

Underneath the ancient trees,
Strings vibrate with the forest's love.
Laughter mingles with the breeze,
As stars twinkle from above.

Each note a petal kissed by air,
In every heart, the music flows.
In this realm, without a care,
Joy and wonder freely grows.

So let your spirit twirl and sway,
In the faerie's ethereal tune.
For every moment's bright display,
Is a gift beneath the moon.

Sonorous Dreams in Faerie Light

In twilight's glow, the shadows play,
Whispers weave where fairies sway.
Each star that twinkles, softly calls,
Dreams arise as night enthralls.

Glistening dew on emerald blades,
Magic shimmer, the darkness fades.
Chiming laughter echoes near,
Holding secrets we revere.

Underneath the ancient trees,
Floating softly on the breeze.
Enchanted visions, pure delight,
In vivid hues of faerie light.

Threads of Enchantment and Grace

Silken threads spun by the moon,
Weaving stories, sweet and soon.
Echoes linger, soft and clear,
In this realm, your heart draws near.

Glimmers dance on petals fair,
Every whisper, a tender care.
Dreams entwined within the night,
All is lost in purest light.

Curled in shadows, secrets dwell,
Each heartbeat casts a gentle spell.
With every breath, the magic flows,
In nature's arms, true beauty grows.

The Dance of Elfin Echoes

In moonlit glades, the fairies twirl,
With laughter bright, their hair a whirl.
Clad in shimmer, they take flight,
In the stillness of the night.

Leaves a-flutter, soft perfume,
Filling the air with joy's sweet bloom.
Elfin echoes, rich and bold,
Stories whispered, ages told.

As starlit paths begin to weave,
A tapestry of dreams to leave.
With every step, enchantments glow,
In the dance, their spirits flow.

Nocturnal Murmurs of the Sylvan Spire

Beneath the boughs of ancient tree,
Nocturnal murmurs set us free.
In shadows deep where secrets sigh,
Time stands still, as stars drift by.

Whispers carried on the air,
Echoes rise, dissolving care.
Softly gliding through the night,
Holding dreams in gentle light.

Mystic pathways, moonlit trails,
Where every heart and spirit sails.
With each pulse, the forest breathes,
In every sigh, a world it weaves.

Arcane Harmonies of the Night

In shadows deep, secrets reside,
Whispers flutter, secrets abide.
Moonlight dances on ancient trees,
Mysteries carried by the breeze.

Stars glimmer like a distant choir,
Strumming hearts with soft desire.
Night unfurls its velvet cloak,
In the silence, the stars spoke.

Echoes linger in twilight's breath,
Tales of love and whispers of death.
Arcane tales in the air do weave,
In every sigh, the night believes.

Beneath the gaze of watchful eyes,
In the realm where the silence lies.
Enchanting melodies float and sway,
In the night, all hearts will play.

Luminous Notes on the Wing

In the dawn's light, a song takes flight,
Melodies soaring, pure delight.
Feathers brushed with hues so rare,
Nature's symphony fills the air.

Voices blend in harmonious throng,
Each winged creature sings its song.
Sun-kissed notes on the gentle breeze,
Charming hearts beneath the trees.

A whisper of joy in every trill,
Brings the heart a fragrant thrill.
Dancing to rhythms, life anew,
In the songbird's world, joy shines through.

Songs of hope, woven so fine,
Brighten the world, a love divine.
Luminous notes in the morning glow,
Guide our hearts where dreams may flow.

Songs of the Faerie Court

In glades where whispers softly beckon,
Faeries spin tales, delight, and reckon.
With gossamer wings and laughter bright,
They dance 'neath the stars in the soft moonlight.

Each note they sing, a magical spell,
Binding the hearts where the shadows dwell.
Songs of joy, of longing, of play,
In the faerie court, where night meets day.

Ringlets of laughter ride on the wind,
Stories of old, eternally pinned.
With flickering starlight, they weave and twine,
In the echo of laughter, all hearts align.

From thistle and bloom, they gather their tunes,
Enchanted by silver, illuminated moons.
A celebration that never shall cease,
In the faerie court, all find their peace.

Echoes Between the Veils

Veils of time whisper soft and low,
Carried by currents where shadows flow.
In the spaces where silence dwells,
Echoes emerge with magical spells.

Threads of the past entwine the now,
Mysteries linger, they wonder how.
Through ages lost, voices call,
Reverberating through the eternal hall.

Softly echoing, the spirits sing,
A haunting melody, whispers cling.
Between the realms, they softly sway,
Guiding lost souls along their way.

In the twilight, where shadows blend,
Each echo carries a tale to send.
Between the veils, the secrets stay,
In every heartbeat, come what may.

The Dance of Ethereal Echoes

In twilight's glow, we sway and twirl,
Each step a whisper, soft and swirl.
Echoes of laughter fill the air,
With every note, we shed our care.

The music beckons, spirits soar,
From hidden realms, they seek the floor.
A timeless waltz, both near and far,
In shadows cast by the evening star.

Gliding softly, the ethereal throng,
Drawn to the rhythm, sweet and strong.
Moments entwined in the night so bright,
As dreams unfold in the pale moonlight.

Hands clasped tight, we merge as one,
In harmony till the night is done.
The dance of echoes, endless flight,
A fleeting glimpse of pure delight.

Starlit Melodies in Whispering Woods

In the woods where secrets lie,
Starlit melodies float and sigh.
Leaves murmur songs of ages past,
Carried by winds that whisper fast.

Beneath the boughs, the shadows play,
Where echoes of night softly sway.
Moonbeams weave through the branches high,
Painting dreams as soft winds sigh.

Crickets chirp a symphony sweet,
With rustling leaves in rhythmic beat.
Nature's chorus, a tranquil sound,
In the heart of the woods, peace is found.

Stars gaze down on this sacred glade,
Illuminating the serenade.
Every note, a lullaby true,
In starlit woods, under skies so blue.

Ribbons of Light and Shadow

Dancing ribbons in twilight's embrace,
Light and shadow in a delicate race.
Flashes of gold, hues of deep gray,
Weaving a tale as night turns to day.

Branches arch like fingers of fate,
Holding the moments, the hours, the weight.
A tapestry spun with silken threads,
Stories of dreams as the daylight spreads.

Frosted whispers in the early dawn,
Promises linger as shadows yawn.
The world awakens in a gentle sigh,
With ribbons of color that grace the sky.

Each hue a memory, ephemeral flight,
Painting the canvas of day from night.
Eagerly woven, each shade a part,
Of the eternal dance within the heart.

Secrets of the Faery Lyre

In the glen where the faeries play,
A lyre is strummed at the end of day.
Each note a secret, soft and clear,
Inviting all who wander near.

With plucked strings, the tales arise,
Of ancient woods and starlit skies.
Whispers carried on a gentle breeze,
Echoing dreams among the trees.

Laughter twinkles in the moon's pale light,
As shadows gather and take to flight.
Melodies wrapped in silken folds,
Revealing wonders that time upholds.

The faery's song, a call to the brave,
Inviting hearts beyond the grave.
In its embrace, we lose and find,
The secrets woven in the mind.

The Melody of Moonlit Enclave

In shadows deep, where whispers play,
The silver beams lead hearts astray.
Gently swaying, the willows weave,
Old secrets held, in night's reprieve.

A chorus soft, in twilight's fold,
Echoes of stories, waiting, untold.
With every note, the stars align,
Creating magic, both yours and mine.

The breeze carries tunes, sweet as wine,
Dancing dreams in this realm divine.
Under the gaze of the watchful sky,
In this enclave, together, we fly.

Dulcet Dreams under Starry Canopy

Beneath the vast, enchanted sphere,
Where constellations softly cheer.
The lullabies of night entwine,
In dreams that shimmer, bright and fine.

Dark velvet skies cradle our thoughts,
Each star a wish, that fate begot.
With every breath, serenity grows,
In the stillness, the heart knows.

Floating through realms of pure delight,
Safety found in the cloak of night.
Whispers of peace, the cosmos sings,
While gently cradling our tender wings.

Meandering through the Dreaming Glades

Winding pathways pave the way,
Where ancient trees in silence sway.
A vivid tapestry unfolds,
In every glade, a tale that molds.

The leaves converse in gentle sighs,
As dappled sunlight bathes our eyes.
Each step unveils a hidden grace,
In the quietness of this place.

Footprints cushioned by mossy beds,
Among the ferns where magic spreads.
Whisked away on nature's breath,
In dreaming glades, we dance with death.

The Fable of Resonant Sylphs

In whispers soft, the sylphs call,
Their laughter echoes, a silken thrall.
Through gossamer veils, they flit and play,
Spinning legends in twilight's sway.

With every flutter, secrets shared,
The heart awakens, unprepared.
A melody woven through air so light,
Calling us forth, into the night.

Among the stars, they weave their fate,
In realms where dreams and wishes await.
Boundless spirits, forever they drift,
Carrying magic, a celestial gift.

Tremors of the Twilight Symphony

In the fading light we linger slow,
Whispers of dusk begin to glow.
A melody woven of dreams untold,
Each heartbeat echoes, soft and bold.

Stars awaken in the darkened sky,
Drawing us near with a gentle sigh.
The twilight hums a haunting tune,
As shadows dance beneath the moon.

Fingers brush through the evening air,
Carrying secrets that we both share.
With every note, our spirits entwine,
Lost in a rhythm so divine.

Time stretches thin, then slips away,
In this symphony where night meets day.
We sway like leaves on a restless breeze,
Captured in magic, moments freeze.

As twilight fades to a velvet night,
We hold onto echoes of fading light.
In the silence, a promise abides,
In the depths of the heart, love resides.

Enigmatic Strains in the Moon's Caress

Under the moon's soft silver glare,
Mysteries linger, dissolve in the air.
Each note a raindrop, a pulse in the dark,
A song of enchantment, igniting a spark.

Waves of emotion crash on the shore,
While shadows beckon, inviting us more.
With every whisper, the night unfolds,
Stories of longing, of truth untold.

Time slows down in this timeless place,
As we wander through longing's embrace.
The strains intertwine, a delicate thread,
Binding our spirits, where dreams have led.

A dance of reflection in moon's embrace,
Unraveled secrets, a lover's chase.
With each gentle stroke of the midnight breeze,
We surrender to fate, with hearts at ease.

In the quiet hour, a promise born,
Amidst the laughter, the dreams, the scorn.
We weave our tales in silvery beams,
In the depths of the night, we chase our dreams.

The Murmur of Enchanted Spheres

In a garden where starlight sways,
The universe hums in mystic ways.
Each breath a whisper, each touch a song,
The dance of the cosmos, where we belong.

Voices of planets, a soft refrain,
Carried by winds, it calls our name.
As comets streak through the velvet night,
We close our eyes and embrace the light.

Cradled in orbit, our spirits soar,
Exploring realms where we yearn for more.
The gravitational pull of dreams so bright,
Drawing us deeper into the night.

Fleeting moments, like shooting stars,
We hold forever in our hearts.
The murmur enchants, a timeless crest,
In the sphere of wonder, we find our rest.

As infinity whispers in sacred tones,
We find meaning, where love atones.
In this cosmic dance, we shall remain,
Bound by the music, the joy, the pain.

Notes of Illusion and Wonder

In a world where shadows weave,
Fragments of light start to deceive.
Each note a flicker, a spark divine,
Illusions dance, like aged wine.

Time spins tales in a fleeting glance,
Creating a moment, a daring chance.
With every heartbeat, a new refrain,
A tapestry woven from joy and pain.

We wander through dreams, hand in hand,
In a landscape crafted by night's command.
Echoes of laughter, shadows of past,
In this fleeting world, we drift and cast.

As twilight envelops, the silence sings,
Notes of wonder on whispered wings.
Together we lose ourselves in the glow,
Of possibilities, forever flow.

In the truth of illusions, we find our place,
Caught in the beauty of time and space.
In the heart of wonder, we dare to believe,
That magic resides in all we perceive.

Reverberations of Forgotten Tales

In shadows deep, the stories fade,
Echoes dance on time's parade.
Whispers linger in the night,
Veils of memory, soft and light.

Lost heroes fade in dreamlike haze,
Their legends told in smoky ways.
The past unfurls, a fragile thread,
Binding hearts where tales have led.

Around the fire, the spirits hum,
Voices low, a gentle drum.
In every word, a spark ignites,
Reviving worlds in quiet nights.

Fleeting moments, a glance exchanged,
Forgotten lore, yet still unchanged.
As time recedes, the tales reside,
Awake within, they softly bide.

In silence strong, we hear the call,
Of ancient echoes, one and all.
With every heartbeat, stories weave,
In reverberations, we believe.

The Faery Flute's Allure

In twilight's grace, a tune takes flight,
A faery's flute, in silver light.
Soft melodies weave through the trees,
Whispers sweet, carried on the breeze.

Dancing shadows, a nocturnal show,
The moonlit path where dreamers go.
With every note, the world transforms,
In melodies, the heart conforms.

Glimmers spark in the night's embrace,
The faery's song, a timeless grace.
Wanderers pause, enchanted there,
Caught in the magic of the air.

A playful laugh rings fresh and clear,
As stars twinkle, drawing near.
The flute's allure, a siren's call,
Where shadows cast and spirits fall.

With each refrain, the night expands,
A world alive at the faery's hands.
In gentle tones, our worries cease,
In the flute's embrace, we find our peace.

Ghostly Notes in the Glistening Gloom

In the hush of night, whispers flow,
Ghostly notes in a silver glow.
Through misty air, they gently fade,
Echoes of dreams that softly played.

The shadows sway like waves of time,
In spectral dance, a haunting rhyme.
Lurking thoughts in the glistening dark,
Filling hearts with a fleeting spark.

Veils of silence, a spectral veil,
With secrets woven, the stories sail.
In every sigh, a tale untold,
Of loves once cherished, now turned cold.

Notes drift gently on the nightwind's breath,
Whispered memories surrounding death.
In the gloom, where spirits roam,
They find their voice, and call it home.

A serenade from a world unseen,
Crafted in sighs where shadows glean.
In ghostly notes, we find the truth,
Lurking quietly, ageless youth.

Medleys of the Moon's Embrace

Beneath the moon, a soft embrace,
Whispers flow in silver lace.
Glimmering dreams weave through the night,
Carried forth on wings of light.

The stars align in shimmering pools,
Where lovers meet and silence rules.
With every glance, the worlds converge,
In twilight's grace, their souls emerge.

Soft echoes linger, a tender sigh,
In moonlit dance, where shadows lie.
A medley rich, of hearts in bloom,
In the gentle light, dispelling gloom.

A lullaby sung by the nightingale,
Notes that twine like a lover's tale.
With every heartbeat, passion's weave,
In the warmth of night, they won't deceive.

In the moon's embrace, time stands still,
Hearts entwined with the lover's will.
Medleys play on in tender grace,
Forever bound in the moon's embrace.

The Chime of Hidden Realms

In shadows deep, where secrets dwell,
A soft chime calls from beyond the quell.
Mysteries dance in the twilight's grace,
Echoes linger in this sacred space.

Veils of silence gently unwind,
Whispers of worlds that intertwine.
Each note a thread in the cosmic loom,
Weaving tales of life, love, and doom.

Faint glimmers spark in the mind's eye,
A symphony brewed from the sighing sky.
Every heartbeat a pulse from the past,
Resonating memories, shadows cast.

The night unfurls with a graceful hand,
Guiding lost souls to a promised land.
The air is thick with ancient lore,
As echoes beckon from distant shore.

In hidden realms where dreams take flight,
The chime resounds, igniting the night.
A call to hearts with wings unfurled,
To embrace the mystery of the world.

Glimmers of Sound in Dusk's Embrace

As the sun dips low with a fading sigh,
Whispers of dusk begin to fly.
Glimmers of sound in the gentle breeze,
Painting the air like a fragrant tease.

Beneath the boughs where shadows play,
Music lingers at the close of day.
Each rustle a note, each bird a refrain,
A symphony born of joy and pain.

The twilight hums in softest hues,
Every heartbeat a classic muse.
Fading light holds the promise of dreams,
In the quiet where the soul redeems.

Stars ignite in a velvet sky,
A serenade sung, a muted cry.
The world exhales, wrapped in night's shroud,
Silent stories hidden in the crowd.

So linger here in dusk's embrace,
Let the glimmers touch your face.
For every sound that bends the air,
Whispers secrets, gentle and rare.

The Call of the Whispering Winds

The wind awakens with a soft, sweet sigh,
Calling the world, inviting the sky.
With every gust, a story unfolds,
Tales of the earth, ancient and bold.

Whispers carry from mountain peak,
Secrets the silent trees dare not speak.
A chorus of sighs, rustles and calls,
Echoing softly through nature's halls.

Gentle embraces wrap around trees,
Brushing the leaves, dancing with ease.
The call of the winds, a timeless song,
Reminds us of where we all belong.

In the twilight, they swirl and twine,
Through valleys deep and hills divine.
Each breeze a messenger of the night,
Leading lost souls towards the light.

The call persists as the shadows blend,
A journey that never seems to end.
To listen is to truly be free,
United with nature, eternally.

Crescendos in the Velvet Moonlight

Under the gaze of the soft moonlight,
Crescendos rise, cloaked in the night.
A melody woven with silver threads,
In the stillness where the heart treads.

Dreams unfurl like petals in bloom,
Breathing life into the silent gloom.
With every note, shadows dance and play,
As the world turns gently, swaying away.

Stars hum along in a celestial choir,
Igniting the dark with a playful fire.
Each chord a beacon, a guiding star,
Resonating softly, near and far.

In the embrace of this tranquil night,
We surrender to love's pure light.
Crescendos crash like waves on the shore,
Inviting the lost to seek and explore.

So let the moon's magic draw you near,
To a symphony played only for the dear.
In velvet night, our souls take flight,
Crescendos echo, pure delight.

Whispers of Enchanted Harmonies

In twilight's hush, the echoes weave,
Soft sighs of night the stars believe.
Notes of dreams in gentle flight,
Dance in shadows, kiss the night.

A symphony of whispers calls,
Through whispering leaves, where silence falls.
Each heartbeat sways to magic's tune,
Under the watchful, silver moon.

Winds carry secrets, lost and found,
In laughter shared with night's profound.
Voices blend in soft array,
Guiding souls who long to stay.

Harmonies of ancient lore,
Awake the dreams from timeless shore.
Where love's refrain forever stays,
In enchanted nights and starry ways.

With every pulse, a story spun,
The night a canvas, the stars our sun.
In whispers soft, eternity,
A dance of souls forever free.

The Lullaby of Woven Dreams

In shadows deep, the dreams take flight,
Softly sung by stars so bright.
A lullaby for wandering hearts,
As each new night gently imparts.

Woven threads of hopes and fears,
Carried forth on silver veers.
Night's embrace is warm and near,
Whispers cradle, hold us dear.

Through the stillness, spirits glide,
In the realm where dreams abide.
Gentle echoes of the past,
In fragrant night, they ever last.

The moonlight bathes the world in grace,
Cradling us in its warm embrace.
With every sigh, a story flows,
In the slumber where magic grows.

Softly now, the night invites,
To dance beneath the starry lights.
With each heartbeat, dreams entwine,
In this lullaby, forever shine.

Threads of Moonlit Magic

Under the moon's enchanting glow,
Whispers weave where soft winds blow.
Threads of silver in the night,
Linking dreams in soft twilight.

A tapestry of stars above,
Touched by whispered tales of love.
Each moment spun like gossamer,
Binding hearts that drift and stir.

In night's embrace, the magic sways,
As gentle breezes softly play.
We dance along this cosmic thread,
Where dreams are born and softly spread.

With every stitch, new worlds arise,
In the fabric where silence lies.
Moonlit secrets softly breathe,
In the dreams that night conceives.

As dawn approaches, colors blend,
Yet magic lingers, never end.
In every heart, a light remains,
From moonlit threads, our joy sustains.

Tides of Celestial Serenades

In the distance, waves of light,
Surge as day gives way to night.
Celestial currents softly flow,
In serenades of stars aglow.

Under sky, we find our peace,
As the universe whispers, release.
The tides of time sweep us along,
In harmony with the cosmic song.

Every note a gentle wave,
Ebbing feelings, hearts to save.
With each rise, a hope takes form,
In every lull, the world is warm.

As constellations lead the way,
We wander through the night's ballet.
The ocean sings its timeless tune,
Beneath the watchful, timeless moon.

In the stillness, dreams ignite,
In starlit whispers, pure delight.
Tides carry us to shores unknown,
Celestial serenades, our own.

Whispers of Enchanted Threads

In twilight's hush, secrets weave,
Silent stories, dreams believe,
With each thread, magic flows,
Woven tales only night knows.

Stars above begin to gleam,
Guiding hearts to softly dream,
Fingers dance in gentle light,
Crafting visions through the night.

A tapestry of whispered dreams,
Glimmers bright in silver beams,
Every stitch, a wish to send,
In this realm where realms blend.

Enchantments hum in the air,
Lifting spirits beyond compare,
In fibers spun from ancient lore,
The heart seeks what it longs for.

As dawn threatens to break through,
The threads unspool, lost from view,
Yet in dreams, they will remain,
In our hearts, the magic's gain.

Lullabies from the Hidden Grove

In shadows deep, a cradle sways,
Where soft winds sing through leafy bays,
Gentle verses fill the night,
Wrapping souls in peace and light.

Crickets chirp a soothing tune,
Underneath the silver moon,
Embers glow on mossy walls,
Nature's lullaby calls and calls.

Branches sway, a whispered prayer,
A promise made on the night's air,
Close your eyes, let worries cease,
In the grove, you'll find your peace.

Dreams imbue the tranquil trees,
Fluttering gently with the breeze,
Hidden spells in every sound,
In this haven, love is found.

Tomorrow brings the dawn's soft glow,
But for now, let sweet dreams flow,
In the grove of secrets told,
Lullabies weave hearts of gold.

Melodies of the Charmed Canopy

Beneath the branches, stories sing,
Of magic woven in the spring,
Birds take flight with joyful cries,
As the sun paints the azure skies.

Leaves shimmer with a silken grace,
Each rustle tells a warm embrace,
Nature's music, soft and light,
Guides us deeper into night.

Whispers blend with breezes fair,
Carrying dreams through fragrant air,
A symphony of life we feel,
Every note a truth to heal.

In this dance, the spirits twirl,
Around the world, they gracefully swirl,
A harmony for hearts to share,
In the canopy, love's song is rare.

As stars emerge with golden glow,
Melodies ebb and softly flow,
Underneath this magical span,
We find the beauty of life's plan.

Echoes Beneath the Moonlit Glade

In the glade where shadows play,
Moonlight guides the lost astray,
Echoes of the night's refrain,
Drawing hearts to feel the pain.

Mysteries whisper through the trees,
Carried by the midnight breeze,
Each sound a story to unfold,
Of ancient truth and tales retold.

Footsteps soft on the mossy floor,
Take us to the dreamer's door,
Where the night's secrets convene,
In the silence, sights unseen.

Stars watch over as we tread,
In the glade, our spirits wed,
With echoes merging, hopes ascend,
In this space, all paths bend.

As the dawn begins to break,
The shadows fade, and hearts awake,
Yet forever will the echoes stay,
Beneath the moonlit glade, we play.

Night's Embrace in Gentle Cadence

Underneath the silver glow,
Stars are dancing, soft and slow.
Moonlight weaves a tender spell,
In the quiet, hearts do dwell.

Shadows weave through ancient trees,
Carried softly by the breeze.
Whispers linger, dreams take flight,
Wrapped in peace of velvet night.

Crickets sing of love and loss,
Time it seems has no true cost.
Every breath a lullaby,
Beneath the blanket of the sky.

Glimmers of the dawn approach,
Yet the night will always coach.
Rest in warmth till morn appears,
In the dark, we cast our fears.

Musings of Faery Song

In the glen where shadows play,
Faeries dance at close of day.
With a laugh, the night awakes,
In the echoes, music breaks.

Tiny lights like fireflies,
Twirl and whirl beneath the skies.
Magic whispers through the leaves,
In the heart, a spirit weaves.

Every note a tale to tell,
Of secret worlds where wishes dwell.
Softly sung on gentle breeze,
Hearts find comfort, souls find ease.

In the silence, dreams will rise,
From the depths, our hopes will fly.
With a gleam of stardust bright,
Embrace the faery's song tonight.

Cadence of the Whispering Leaves

Rustling softly in the night,
Leaves converse in pure delight.
Each one carries tales untold,
Of the warmth and winter's cold.

Branches sway with ancient grace,
Nature's rhythm, time and space.
In their dance, a story flows,
Echoes of what nature knows.

Glimmers of the sun's soft kiss,
Hidden in the morning mist.
With each whisper, songs unfold,
In the leaves, the world turns gold.

Every gust, a fleeting thought,
In a language long forgot.
Listen close, for wisdom's there,
In the cadence of the air.

The Wistful Call of Forgotten Woods

In the depths of shadowed glade,
Whispers linger, softly fade.
Lost are tales of days gone by,
Where the stillness bends and sighs.

Mossy stones and crumbling twigs,
Mark the paths of weary digs.
Echoes of the past remain,
In the heart, a tender pain.

Every tree a sentinel,
Guarding secrets, dreams compel.
Ghosts of laughter, memories,
Every whisper rides the breeze.

Wistful calls through leafy veils,
Guide the wanderer with tales.
In these woods, the spirits play,
Longing for the light of day.

A Tapestry of Enchanted Notes

In twilight's glow, the whispers weave,
Melodies of dreams, that we believe.
The notes dance lightly on the breeze,
Painting the night with gentle ease.

Each string plucked sings a tale of old,
A harmony of hearts, brave and bold.
The echoes linger, softly spun,
Binding us close, as one begun.

Through moonlit paths, the music plays,
Guiding lost souls in winding ways.
With every chord, our spirits rise,
A tapestry bright against dark skies.

In enchanted realms where secrets lay,
The notes entwine, come what may.
A harmony forged by fate's sweet hand,
Together we stand, in this mystical land.

So let us dance in the silken night,
Drawn by the pull of pure delight.
For in this moment, we are free,
A tapestry of love, just you and me.

The Symphony Beneath the Stars

Under the canvas of the night,
Sounds of the cosmos take their flight.
Every twinkle, a note so bright,
Creating symphonies of pure delight.

The crickets chirp, a soothing tune,
While the owls call to the silver moon.
In the serene hush, we find our place,
Lost in the rhythm of time and space.

The winds carry whispers of ancient lore,
As starlight shimmers on the forest floor.
Nature's chorus, both wild and free,
A melody of life, eternally.

With every heartbeat, the night unfolds,
Stories of passion, of bravery bold.
In this symphony beneath the skies,
Our spirits soar, as dreams arise.

So let us listen and let us feel,
The magic that night cannot conceal.
For in the dark, together we find,
The symphony of the heart and mind.

Woven Echoes in Ancient Woods

Amidst the trees where shadows play,
A sacred space where echoes sway.
Each rustling leaf sings of the past,
In whispers soft, a bond held fast.

The ancient boughs, they bend and sway,
Guardians of secrets that will not fray.
In the stillness, time stands still,
Binding our hearts with nature's will.

Through ages long, the echoes call,
Stories of life, of rise and fall.
Woven tales on the gentle breeze,
Carried through branches, rustling leaves.

With every step on the mossy ground,
The pulse of history can be found.
In the thickets deep, a magic stirs,
A symphony only nature hears.

So wander softly, heed the song,
In ancient woods where we belong.
For woven echoes will ever bind,
Our souls to the earth and the divine.

The Lyric of Lost Spirits

In the quiet dusk, where shadows blend,
Echoes of lost souls start to send.
The lyric weaves through the still air,
A haunting tune of love and despair.

They dance like whispers on a breeze,
Carrying tales of lifelong pleas.
Each note a memory, softly worn,
A serenade for hearts left torn.

In moonlight's grasp, their shadows twirl,
Lost spirits drift in a timeless whirl.
The melodies linger, sweet and low,
A song of sorrow, a tale of woe.

Yet from the depths of longing's embrace,
Rises a chorus, a sacred grace.
For even the lost, in time, shall find,
A lyric that forever binds.

So listen closely in the night's dark hue,
To the song that calls out, warm and true.
For the lyric of lost spirits will impart,
The beauty of love, forever in the heart.

Songbirds in the Realm of Shadows

In twilight's embrace, they softly sing,
Notes that wander, like dreams on the wing.
Echoes intertwine in the dusky air,
Whispers of hope, woven with care.

Perched on branches, hearts take flight,
Painting the dusk with vibrant light.
Their melodies chase the shadows away,
Banish the night, welcome the day.

Through silence and song, a bond they weave,
In every note, a tale to believe.
Listen closely, let their chorus rise,
In this shadowed realm, beauty lies.

Each flitting form, a spirit set free,
Carving stories in the canopy.
With every flutter, they share their grace,
In the realm of shadows, they find their place.

Songbirds in twilight, a fleeting sight,
Guiding lost souls through the night.
Together they soar, above and beyond,
In harmony's arms, they graciously respond.

Harmony's Breath Between Worlds

Between the worlds, a sweet refrain,
Soft as whispers, light as rain.
In hidden groves, where shadows dance,
Harmony's breath, a fleeting chance.

Colors entwine in the gentle breeze,
Songs of the heart, where spirits please.
Mingling echoes, a sacred sound,
Uniting the lost, where peace is found.

Glimmers of hope, like fireflies' flight,
Illuminate paths in the deepening night.
In every sigh, eternity waits,
Wisdom of ages, as time creates.

Cascading notes in the twilight glow,
From heart to heart, the music flows.
In stillness, we find the world's embrace,
Harmony's breath, a timeless grace.

Between the worlds, let spirits soar,
In unison, let us explore.
Together we weave a tapestry bright,
Harmony's pulse, a guiding light.

Atonal Whispers in a Faerie Glint

Through the glades, soft whispers roam,
Atonal echoes, far from home.
In faerie lights that flicker and sway,
Mysteries linger, come what may.

Glimmers of laughter in the cool night air,
Atonal chimes create a snare.
Woven in shadows, enchantments spin,
In every breath, a world points within.

Fleeting moments, like dust in time,
Gentle voices, a forgotten rhyme.
In the distance, shadows converse,
A song of wonder, life's universe.

Characters weave in ephemeral light,
Each one a story, a day turned to night.
In whimsical tunes, we seek and we find,
Atonal whispers, forever entwined.

Faerie realms call on the heart's embrace,
In the quietude, a sacred space.
With wavering notes, we spiral, we spin,
In the magic of night, let enchantments begin.

The Serenade of Gossamer Voices

In twilight's curtain, soft and thin,
Gossamer voices beckon within.
They dance on the air, like whispers of silk,
Caressing the moonlight, as sweet as milk.

Silhouetted dreams in the calm of night,
Serenading stars that shine so bright.
Echoes of laughter, a delicate song,
Gossamer threads where we all belong.

With every breath, a memory shared,
Soft serenades of those who cared.
In the silence between, the stories unfold,
Whispers of love that never grow old.

Fluttering gently, the voices arise,
Painting the heavens with lullabies.
In their embrace, we find our peace,
The serenade flows, a gentle release.

Tangled in dreams, in a celestial dance,
Gossamer voices invite us to glance.
At the tapestry woven with threads of delight,
In this serenade, all hearts take flight.

Whisked Away by Faerie Soundscapes

In twilight's glow, they dance and sway,
Whispers of magic, lead me away.
Misty trees with secrets to share,
Glimmers of light float through the air.

Songs of the brook, soft as a sigh,
Calling me close, as shadows fly.
Fluttering wings, a delicate scheme,
Lost in the fabric of a woven dream.

Moonbeams spin notes of silver and gold,
Here, within wonders, my heart feels bold.
Captured in melodies, soft and profound,
Enchanted, I'm whisked by faerie sound.

Laughter erupts from the depths of the glade,
The rhythmic pulse of bliss is laid.
Through ages past, an echo streams,
Time intertwines with the threads of dreams.

A symphony calls from the heart of the night,
Where whispers of wonder ignite pure delight.
And here I will linger, with faeries in view,
In soundscapes of magic, forever anew.

Dreaming in Resonant Paths

In the quiet dew of morning's light,
Dreams take flight in brilliant sight.
Waves of color stretch through the air,
Each vibrant note scattered with care.

With every step on calmed, warm sand,
Footprints of wishes emerge, hand in hand.
Echoes of laughter, a sweet serenade,
Blending with nature, our fears start to fade.

Winding through forests where soft shadows play,
Whispers of time guide us on our way.
Resonant paths weave a delicate thread,
Leading us forth where our spirits are fed.

A tapestry rich, in colors so deep,
Awakening dreams as we drift into sleep.
In the heart of a world where wishes collide,
We find the serenity together, inside.

Journeys unraveled in songs of the night,
As each note expands, shaping new light.
Together we wander, forever in tune,
Dreaming in paths that dance 'neath the moon.

The Lingering Sigh of Hidden Harmonies

In shadows cast by the fading sun,
Whispers reside, a world just begun.
Echoes of longing drift through the trees,
Harmonies hidden, carried by the breeze.

With every heartbeat, hope takes its flight,
Gentle vibrations, soft as the night.
Sighs intertwine with the breath of the earth,
Filling each moment with magical worth.

Notes undulate in the fabric of time,
Serenading secrets in whispers and chime.
The world sways softly to an unseen song,
Mapping the path where we all belong.

Hidden reflections dance in the dark,
Awake in the silence, we find the spark.
A beautiful linger, the breath of a dream,
In sighs of the evening, harmonies gleam.

So here we remain, in twilight's embrace,
Listening deep to the sounds, time won't erase.
The lingering sigh spreads its wings wide,
Inviting our souls to tenderly glide.

Tantalizing Lyricism of the Unknown

Beyond the horizon, where shadows twine,
Lies the allure of the whispers divine.
Unraveled stories beckon the brave,
In tantalizing tones from the depths of the wave.

Rhythms of silence pulse in the night,
Breath of the cosmos igniting the light.
Hidden adventures await with a call,
As echoes of wonders softly enthrall.

Uncharted routes laced with vibrant glow,
Twisty paths holding the magic we know.
Each note a compass to wander the soul,
And lyrics unravel the mysteries whole.

With every heartbeat, the unknown unveils,
The dance of existence, where spirit prevails.
Tantalizing dreams in the depth of the night,
Whispering truths in the cosmic delight.

So here in the shadows, let your heart roam,
The lyricism calls, leading us home.
In the realm of the unseen, we're free to explore,
Tantalizing whispers keep urging for more.

Echoing Lullabies in Timeless Realms

Whispers of dreams in twilight's grace,
Softly they linger in a sacred space.
Stars twinkle gently, a cosmic song,
Echoing lullabies where hearts belong.

A world so quiet, wrapped in embrace,
Time dances slowly, setting the pace.
Ethereal shadows play on the ground,
In timeless realms, pure solace is found.

Each note a promise, a tender refrain,
Woven with love through joy and pain.
In shimmering silence, the night takes flight,
Guiding lost souls through endless night.

Emotions unspoken, a gentle sigh,
As dreams intertwine beneath the sky.
In the lull of the cosmos, we drift and sway,
Together we wander, come what may.

The Caress of Moonlit Harmonies

In the hush of dusk, a melody calls,
Soft as the shimmer that gently falls.
Moonlit whispers wrap around the night,
Caressing our spirits, setting them alight.

Chords of the cosmos, in sync we breathe,
Golden threads of magic, a tapestry we weave.
As shadows dance lightly, in rhythmic play,
The sun bows gracefully, yielding the day.

Each note intertwined with the breeze's sigh,
Cradle our dreams as they softly fly.
In the arms of the night, let our hearts take wing,
United in harmony, together we sing.

With every heartbeat, the world stands still,
As the moon casts its shadows with gentle will.
In this sacred moment, we lose our way,
In the caress of music, forever we stay.

Dance of Shadows and Luminous Strings

In the twilight's glow, shadows pirouette,
Strings hum a tune we shan't forget.
With every heartbeat, the night unfolds,
Stories of magic in whispers retold.

Beneath a canopy of stars we sway,
Lost in the rhythm, we drift away.
Each flicker of light a spark of delight,
As shadows embrace us in soft moonlight.

The winds carry whispers of dreams yet unknown,
In a dance of shadows, we've brightly shone.
As laughter cascades like a gentle stream,
We surrender ourselves to the night's sweet dream.

With luminous strings, our souls intertwine,
A tapestry woven, both yours and mine.
In the warm embrace of this endless night,
Together we flourish, our hearts take flight.

The Harmonious Veil of the Enchanted Night

A veil of wonder, the night adorns,
As magic unfolds with the rise of the dawns.
Crickets serenade under the stars,
Wrapped in a harmony that heals our scars.

Night blooms with secrets, in shadows they play,
Guardians of dreams as we drift away.
The moon lends its light with a gentle sigh,
Illuminating pathways where enchantments lie.

In the hush of twilight, stories are spun,
Of battles and glories, of love never done.
Each flickering star, a spark of delight,
In the harmonious veil of the enchanted night.

With every soft whisper, the cosmos aligns,
Binding our spirits in starlit designs.
As time softly lingers, we lose our way,
In the veil of night, forever we stay.

Harmonic Flickers in a Gilded Glade

In the sunlight's gentle play,
Whispers dance on leaves so light,
Melodies of joy convey,
Nature sings from dawn till night.

Colors twirl in crisp, clean air,
Petals flutter, soft and bright,
Harmony is everywhere,
Gilded glimmers spark delight.

Beams of gold through branches weave,
Casting shadows, swift and fleet,
Every moment we believe,
Time in stillness finds its beat.

Echoes of a soft refrain,
Call the heart to pause and feel,
Joyful tunes and sweet, sweet pain,
In this glade, the soul can heal.

Beneath the arch of emerald,
Peace unfolds as senses bloom,
In this place where dreams are told,
We find solace, love, and room.

Swaying in the Realm of Dreams

In twilight's soft embrace we sway,
Floating lightly, hearts aglow,
Tales of night guide us away,
To a place where whispers flow.

Stars above like lanterns gleam,
Lighting shadows, brief and kind,
In this realm, we weave our dream,
Time dissolves, our cares unwind.

Gentle breezes kiss our cheeks,
Cocooned in silence, sweet, divine,
Here in stillness, solace speaks,
Every heartbeat, every line.

Lost within this magic sway,
Where the dark holds secrets deep,
In the night, we cease to stray,
Catching dreams, as worlds now leap.

We twirl in realms of silent grace,
Among the stars, hand in hand,
Beneath the cosmos, we embrace,
Swaying softly, unplanned.

The Lattice of Luminous Lullabies

In the hush of night, we find,
Threads of light, a silver thread,
Lullabies to soothe the mind,
Guiding dreams where few have tread.

Stars weave songs through velvet skies,
Notes that shimmer, soft and bright,
Each twinkling, a sweet surprise,
Binding hearts with purest light.

Winds of change, a tender breeze,
Carry whispers from afar,
Cradling hopes with greatest ease,
Anchored by the evening star.

In this lattice, dreams unite,
Sculpted by both joy and pain,
Moments painted pure and bright,
Holding laughter, love's sweet reign.

Let the night wrap round us tight,
As lullabies in chorus soar,
In this realm of shining light,
Forever bound, forevermore.

Silken Strains in the Sylvan Deep

In the forest's heart, we roam,
Silken strains of life do weave,
Echoing through nature's dome,
We find solace, hearts believe.

Every leaf a note, a sound,
Rustling softly in the breeze,
Harmony in colors found,
Melodies of ancient trees.

Beneath the boughs, the world awakes,
Whispers dance among the roots,
In this depths, the heart forsakes,
Every sorrow, joy salutes.

Rivers hum their tender tune,
Crickets join in distant choir,
Night reveals a silver moon,
Igniting every deep desire.

Among the trunks, we feel the pulse,
Of life that thrives and grows anew,
In this sylvan, sweet convulse,
Silken strains beckon, loud and true.

Celestial Chimes of the Arcane Wood

In the heart where shadows play,
Whispers of the night ballet.
Moonlight drapes the ancient trees,
Softly sighing with the breeze.

Ethereal tones begin to weave,
Caressing dreams that dare believe.
Stars align in harmony,
A tune of pure serenity.

Branches sway with gentle grace,
Echoes of a timeless place.
Mystic glimmers dance around,
In this sacred woodland sound.

Each note brings a tale untold,
Of the brave and the bold.
Together they create a song,
Where the heart and soul belong.

So listen close, and let it guide,
As celestial chimes abide.
In the arcane wood we find,
Peace and magic intertwined.

Elysian Notes Under Starlit Arches

Beneath the vast celestial dome,
Elysian notes lead us home.
Whispers float on twilight air,
Creating dreams beyond compare.

Each star a beacon, bright and true,
Blending hearts with midnight's hue.
Melodies of love and light,
Dance in shadows of the night.

Arching skies, a symphony,
Of hopes and wishes, wild and free.
The universe in perfect tune,
Embraces all beneath the moon.

In the stillness, magic brews,
With every note, we are renew.
Feel the pulse of ancient lore,
As we open each hidden door.

In harmony, our spirits blend,
As Elysian notes transcend.
Together we shall weave and soar,
Under starlit arches evermore.

The Soft Touch of Enchantment's Muse

In the hush of evening's glow,
Whispers ride where soft winds blow.
Enchantment's muse takes gentle flight,
Drawing dreams from deepest night.

With tender hands, it weaves a tale,
As silver threads begin to pale.
Each brush of grace, a lullaby,
Sings of wonders soaring high.

Ripples of time, a fleeting dance,
Invite the heart to take a chance.
In every glance, a promise lies,
Beneath the starlit, velvet skies.

Fleeting shadows, soft like dew,
Carry secrets, old and new.
A spell of love, pure and bright,
Guides us through the silent night.

So let us wander, hand in hand,
In enchantment's gentle land.
Where the soft touch opens wide,
The infinite dreams that reside.

Resonance of the Dreaming Fae

In twilight's embrace, the Fae arise,
With laughter bright like starlit skies.
Whispers weave through leaf and fern,
As ancient stars begin to turn.

Resonance of their playful song,
Calls the heart to dance along.
Wings of gossamer, light as air,
Paint the night, a canvas rare.

Where forgotten tales are spun anew,
In every dream, their magic grew.
They guide us through the hidden glades,
Where hope and wonder serenades.

Intricate patterns in the night,
Shimmer softly, glowing bright.
In the silence, secrets lie,
As the Fae drift softly by.

With each gentle note they sing,
Awakens hearts to love and spring.
In harmony, let spirits play,
In the resonance of the dreaming Fae.

Harmonies of the Forest's Heart

In the shade where shadows play,
Leaves whisper secrets of the day.
Mossy beds cradle tired feet,
Echoes blend where life is sweet.

Branches sway in rhythmic grace,
Nature's pulse, a tender space.
Birdsong flutters through the air,
A melody beyond compare.

Sunbeams dance on forest floors,
Each moment open wide the doors.
Rustling leaves in soft embrace,
Harmony of time and place.

Roots connect beneath the ground,
Silent stories can be found.
An orchestra of light and shade,
In the forest's heart, unafraid.

Whispers drift on evening's breath,
Starlit skies are life and death.
Yet in the dark, a spark ignites,
The heart of woods, the sound of nights.

Silken Chords of Mystical Realms

In twilight's glow, the shadows play,
Silken chords weave dreams into clay.
Glimmers spark from hidden streams,
We float together, lost in dreams.

Moonlight spills on gentle waves,
The night reveals the heart that craves.
Each note plucked from unseen ties,
Calling forth the stars that rise.

Whispers thread through fabled woods,
Binding tales like ancient hoods.
In the silence, rhythms grow,
Life's sweet pulse, a sacred flow.

Winds carry songs from far and near,
Echoing tales we long to hear.
Mystical realms open wide,
Within the cords, our hopes abide.

In every note, a story's spun,
Each strand reveals the web we've run.
Together we create our fate,
In silken chords, we resonate.

Songs from the Ethereal Boughs

From boughs that stretch towards the sky,
Come whispers soft, a lullaby.
The breeze hums tales of time untold,
In a language of the bold.

Petals dance on gentle air,
Each one sings of love and care.
Sunlit melodies take flight,
Painting dreams in shades of light.

Voices rise in harmonious cheer,
Songs of the heart for all to hear.
Nature's choir, wild and free,
Enchanted notes from every tree.

With every rustle, stories bloom,
In the air, the scent of perfume.
Each song a thread, softly weaved,
In the forest, we believed.

Together we hum, lost in space,
In the boughs, our sacred place.
Ethereal sounds, forever sway,
As we dance through night and day.

The Enigma of Gossamer Serenades

In twilight's embrace, secrets unfold,
Gossamer threads of whispers bold.
Each serenade floats on the breeze,
A fleeting moment that aims to please.

Mysteries linger where shadows weave,
In the night's soft cloak, we believe.
The heart's rhythm syncs with the stars,
Lost in wonder, we mend our scars.

Echoes dance on the edge of dreams,
Fleeting as sunlight on moonlit streams.
A symphony of hope in the air,
Threads of joy, woven with care.

With every note, the silence breaks,
An enigma that softly quakes.
Voices twirl in an intricate game,
A tapestry woven with love's flame.

In the hush, new worlds arise,
Each serenade a sweet surprise.
In the shadows, where secrets rest,
Gossamer dreams become our quest.

Celestial Chords of the Evening Star

Whispers of twilight softly bloom,
Guiding lost dreams toward the moon.
Stars weave tales in silver light,
As night embraces the fading light.

Gentle breezes carry sweet sighs,
Painting the canvas of darkening skies.
Each twinkle a note in the vast expanse,
Inviting the heart to twirl and dance.

Galaxies hum a lullaby's tune,
Echoing softly to the rising moon.
With every chord the cosmos sings,
Awakening magic that evening brings.

Crickets play in harmony's grace,
Nature's rhythm in the sacred space.
As shadows merge with night's embrace,
We find our peace in this tranquil place.

Celestial chords softly entangle,
In the night's grip, our spirits dangle.
A serenade from faraway stars,
Carrying wishes from worlds afar.

The Lure of the Midnight Harp

Under the cloak of a velvet night,
A haunting harp strums pure delight.
Its strings shimmer with ancient lore,
Calling the souls to seek and explore.

Each pluck sends ripples through the dark,
Igniting dreams like a hidden spark.
Echoes dance upon the breeze,
Entwining hearts with graceful ease.

Mysterious notes drift through the air,
Drawing in lovers, the brave, the rare.
In shadows, secrets intertwine,
As melodies weave a story divine.

Soft fingers glide o'er strings so fine,
Singing of hope, where hearts align.
Midnight's spell, a celestial game,
Awakening the wildest flame.

The lure of the harp beckons near,
In twilight whispers, it dries each tear.
Filling the night with sweet, gentle art,
The magic resides in the listening heart.

Dances of Glistening Echoes

In the stillness, echoes arise,
Glistening whispers beneath the skies.
Shimmering sounds like a twinkling stream,
Flowing softly through each waking dream.

They dance among the shadows cast,
An ageless rhythm, a spell that lasts.
Notes twirl and spin, a dazzling sight,
Weaving through silence, capturing light.

Each echo weaves a vibrant tale,
Of whispers shared in a moonlit gale.
Every twang of time, a sacred thread,
In the tapestry of stars overhead.

Dances cradle the slumbering night,
Murmurs of hope, a gentle light.
As the echoes gleam and fade away,
They leave a promise, come what may.

In the great expanse, we find our sway,
Following echoes that lead our way.
Through glistening hints of what's to come,
We join the dance, we've found our home.

The Allure of Ethereal Strings

Beneath the stars, where shadows play,
Ethereal strings begin to sway.
Each note plucked draws the night near,
Inviting all hearts, lost and unclear.

Notes drift like petals on a stream,
Weaving the fabric of every dream.
Softly they beckon, pull us close,
In their embrace, we find our dose.

Through wisps of sound, we are transported,
To realms where every soul is courted.
The allure dances in each refrain,
Binding the joy, releasing the pain.

In twilight's grasp, the strings align,
Creating worlds where love can shine.
With every strum, new stories are spun,
In harmony's grasp, we are all one.

Ethereal strings, like threads of fate,
Unraveling dreams with magic so great.
As dusk wraps around, let us sing,
Embracing the wonder that night will bring.

An Ode to Glimmering Twilight

The sun dips low, a farewell gleam,
Colors blend into a velvet dream.
Stars awake, shy and bright,
Whispers of dusk dance in the light.

Night's embrace, soft and sweet,
Moonbeams kiss the gentle street.
Crickets sing their evening song,
In twilight's glow, where dreams belong.

Fade away the day's warm hue,
Silver streaks and deepening blue.
Silhouette trees against the sky,
In glimmering twilight, time slips by.

A canvas painted with soft sighs,
As constellations begin to rise.
Each star a story, old and new,
In twilight's glow, hope shines through.

So here we pause, let moments linger,
Feel the night's calm, a tender singer.
In glimmering twilight, hearts unite,
Eternal bonds, soft as starlight.

Folly of the Starlight Strains

The night awakens with a gleeful tune,
Stars begin their dance beneath the moon.
Whispers of dreams in the cool night air,
Folly of starlight, casting out despair.

Glimmers twinkle like innocent eyes,
Frivolous wishes ignoring the skies.
In a waltz of chaos, hearts take flight,
Lost in the folly of sweet starlight.

A serenade sung by the shimmering space,
Each note a memory, a fleeting embrace.
Fleeting laughter trapped in time's hold,
Folly of youth in the vibrant bold.

Yet with the dawn, all fades away,
Dreams of the night, in shadows they play.
Lessons of starlight, both cruel and kind,
Folly not forgotten, but left behind.

In silence we ponder, under the sun,
The folly of starlight, it's just begun.
Memories spark in the light of the day,
Echoes of night, in dreams we will stay.

A Symphony of Myth and Mystery

Beneath the moon's glow, legends unfold,
Stories of old, in whispers retold.
Fables entwined with shadows and light,
A symphony beckons, inviting the night.

Creatures of lore in the twilight loom,
Dancing in silence, weaving their room.
Melodies drift on the edge of a sigh,
A harmony lingers beneath the sky.

From forests deep to the mountains high,
Mysteries linger, unseen they lie.
Within the depths where secrets stay,
A symphony plays, guiding the stray.

Each note a heartbeat, a longing glance,
Weaving the tales of our timeless dance.
In the mist, where the wild hearts roam,
Myth and mystery lead us home.

So let us listen to the night's sweet song,
In its embrace, we ever belong.
A symphony of whispers calls us near,
Entwined in wonder, we lose our fear.

The Ethereal Dances of Treetops

In the hush of twilight, branches sway,
Leaves converse in a gentle ballet.
Treetops twirl in the evening breeze,
An ethereal dance, nature's tease.

Moonlight spills on the whispering trees,
Each rustle a note in the night's reprise.
Shadows flicker, a soft mystery,
In the stillness, we find history.

Nature's rhythm, a soft embrace,
Under starlit chandeliers, we trace.
Every rustling leaf, a story told,
In the treetops, magic unfolds.

With every breeze, the world feels right,
Dancing shadows in the silver light.
In this reverie, hearts entwine,
In ethereal dances, we are divine.

So join the waltz of the trees and stars,
Let your spirit soar, let go of scars.
In the treetops, wonder and grace,
Dance with the night, find your place.

The Enchantment of Twinkling Tones

In the stillness of the night,
Soft whispers dance with delight.
Stars above begin to hum,
A melody that pulls us numb.

Gentle breezes carry sound,
From hidden places all around.
Notes collide in playful cheer,
Enchantments sparkle, drawing near.

Moonlit shadows sway and glide,
As time dances, hearts abide.
Every tone a story spun,
In twilight's magic, we are one.

Lingering dreams drift and sway,
In this soft, enchanting play.
Twinkling tones, so sweet and clear,
In the spirit, they draw near.

Sighs of wonder fill the air,
With each sound, a lover's dare.
The night wraps us in its song,
In this world, we all belong.

Veils of Sound in Twilight's Embrace

Veils of sound, like whispers low,
Wrap the dusk in a tender glow.
Crickets chirp a lullaby,
As shadows stretch and softly sigh.

In twilight's warm and hazy shroud,
Nature sings, both bold and proud.
A symphony of leaf and breeze,
In the heart, it brings us ease.

Fireflies twinkle, flicker bright,
Adding magic to the night.
Each note begins to intertwine,
With the heartbeat, pure, divine.

A canvas painted with soft notes,
In gentle waves, the music floats.
Embrace the sound, let it unfold,
In twilight's grip, secrets told.

Hold the moment, sweet and rare,
In the stillness, breathe the air.
Veils of sound, a soft caress,
In twilight's arms, we find our rest.

Chords of the Mystical Grove

In the grove where secrets sleep,
Chords awaken from the deep.
Trees lean in to catch the tune,
Underneath the watchful moon.

Harmony in nature's sway,
Melodies that dance and play.
Branches bow with whispered grace,
Each note holds a soft embrace.

Crimson flowers spin around,
In their petals, echoes found.
Every chord a vibrant thread,
Woven through the air, widespread.

From the silence, music grows,
In the grove, the spirit flows.
Nature's heart in rhythm beats,
In this place, the soul completes.

Lost in time, we softly roam,
In the grove, we find our home.
Chords of magic, wild and free,
In this realm, we come to be.

Echoes of Midnight's Reverie

In the hour of mystic dreams,
Midnight sings in silver beams.
Echoes ripple through the night,
Woven deep with soft moonlight.

Whispers float on twilight's wings,
Lifting hearts with secret things.
Every sound a tender grace,
Wrapped in night's warm, sweet embrace.

Stars above, they twinkle bright,
As shadows dance in the soft light.
Each echo tells a tale so dear,
Carried softly, drawing near.

In the stillness, time suspends,
As the night with magic bends.
Reverie, a gentle flow,
In our hearts, a soft glow.

Cradle dreams, let them unfold,
In the midnight, stories told.
Echoes linger in the air,
In the hush, we find our prayer.

Notes from a Dreamweaver's Harp

In the hush of night, soft strings play,
Echoes of dreams drift far away.
Each note a wish, a tender sigh,
Weaving the stars in a velvet sky.

Whispers of hope in twilight's glow,
Caressing hearts as shadows flow.
With every strum, a story unfurls,
In the tapestry of enchanted worlds.

A gentle breeze carries secrets near,
Lost in the magic, we dance in cheer.
Harp's melody, a guiding light,
Igniting passions through the night.

In silver streams of whispered time,
Dreams intertwine, all rhythms rhyme.
Softly we drift on the music's seam,
Caught in the spell of a woven dream.

As dawn approaches, the notes retreat,
Yet in our souls, they forever beat.
The dreamweaver's harp, a sacred pact,
In every heart, its echo intact.

Glowing Threads of Harmonic Whispers

Threads of light in the silent dusk,
Whispers of hope in every husk.
Melodies entwined like vines of gold,
A vibrant tale gently unfolds.

In the tapestry bright, the colors blend,
Harmonic voices that never end.
Singing softly with rhythmic grace,
In the woven dreams, we find our place.

Notes like raindrops, dancing in air,
Soft serenades that banish despair.
With every heartbeat, a story is spun,
Glowing threads in the warmth of the sun.

Harmonies echo through valleys wide,
Melodic whispers, our hearts abide.
In the silence, let the music grow,
Weaving our fates in a vibrant flow.

Together we rise as the night descends,
Through glowing threads, the journey extends.
In the dreamer's embrace, we softly sway,
Harmonic whispers guide our way.

The Dream Weaver's Celestial Tread

In silver spirals, the dream weaver trod,
Painting the skies with the magic of God.
Footprints of starlight on midnight's veil,
Guiding lost souls through a celestial trail.

Each step a whisper, each breath a song,
Carried on winds, where we all belong.
With threads of creation, we twine and spin,
In the ballroom of dreams, we let love in.

Galaxies shimmer with tales untold,
As night turns to day in hues of gold.
The dream weaver dances to rhythms divine,
A cosmic ballet, a love so fine.

In the heart of the night, the stars align,
Illuminating pathways, a design so fine.
With each fleeting moment, our spirits soar,
In the weaver's realm, we yearn for more.

So let us gather, with hope our thread,
In dreams where we dwell, where fears are shed.
The celestial tread invites us to play,
In the arms of the night, we find our way.

Chasing Shadows with Melodic Light

In twilight's embrace, shadows take flight,
Chasing the echoes of soft, melodic light.
Each note a beacon, guiding our way,
Through the whispering dreams of dusk till day.

Harmony flows in the air we breathe,
Illuminating paths, as we believe.
In the dance of shadows, we find our tune,
As starlit whispers sing to the moon.

The rhythm of night wraps us in peace,
Chasing the fleeting, our worries cease.
In every heartbeat, a symphony wakes,
In the essence of shadows, our joy remakes.

So let the music weave through the fray,
Malodies guiding us, come what may.
A tapestry bright where shadows entwine,
Chasing the echoes of dreams so divine.

In the glow of the night, we rise and roam,
Melodic light leads us gently home.
Through every whisper, we find our sight,
Chasing shadows with melodic light.

www.ingramcontent.com/pod-product-compliance
Ingram Content Group UK Ltd.
Pitfield, Milton Keynes, MK11 3LW, UK
UKHW021530210125
4208UKWH00025B/559

9 781805 599333